STEALING THE DOG'S PROZAC

STEALING THE DOG'S PROZAC

Poems by

Charlotte Lowe

Press 53
Winston-Salem

Press 53
PO Box 30314
Winston-Salem, NC 27130

First Edition

SILVER CONCHO POETRY SERIES
edited by Pamela Uschuk and William Pitt Root

Copyright © 2012 by Charlotte Lowe

All rights reserved, including the right of reproduction in whole or in part in any form. For permission, contact publisher at editor@Press53.com, or at the address above.

Cover design by Kevin Morgan Watson

Cover art Copyright © 2012 by Albert Kogel

Author photo by Mark Rossi

Printed on acid-free paper

ISBN 978-1-935708-51-3

*For my daughter, Faitha,
a boon companion—
good and true—
on the long switchback trail.
This book is for you, with love.*

Acknowledgments

JOURNALS

American Poetry Review: "Last Call For Thwarted Love" (Printed as "The Last One for Thwarted Love")
Changes: "Photo Album"
Country Women: "The Lift"
Cutthroat, A Journal of the Arts: "The Men With Tiny Hands," "Bad Blonde, Lucky Blonde," "Ghost Pass Through" (forthcoming), "Urban Lullaby" (forthcoming)
Hobo Camp Review: "The Matter Is"
The Missing Fez: "Stealing The Dog's Prozac"
Pebble Lake Review: "Tortuga Lovesong"
Ragazine: "Dominoes," "I Dream You Died and You Did," "The Magician's Assistant," "Red Letter"
San Pedro River Review: "Barmaid Rides Herd At The Wagon Wheel" (Spring, 2012)
Texas Portfolio: "Grandma Trying to Die"
Tucson Poet: "Dental Work"

ANTHOLOGIES/PRIZES

Pebble Lake Review Poetry & Fiction Contest award winner: "Tortuga Lovesong"
The Academy of American Poets First Prize: "Silent Marriage"
Tucson Poetry Festival Poetry Prize: "Widowswalk"
The Red Fez Award: "Stealing the Dog's Prozac"
Writers at Work Award, University of Arizona
Tucson Pima Arts Council Creative Writing Fellowship

Contents

Last Call for Thwarted Love	1
Nature of the Beast	2
The Lift	3
Barmaid Rides Herd—At the Wagon Wheel	4
Someone Different Comes Along	5
¡Baile! ¡Baile!	6
They're All About Love	8
No Silver Buckle	10
Oh, Lucky Cows—Grazing Near Big Sur	11
Una Poca De Gracia	13
Sin Zapatos	14
Silent Marriage	15
Dominoes	16
Red Letter	18
Grandma Trying to Die	20
Steps	21
Family Album	22
Ghost Pass Through	23
Ashes, Ashes, We All Fall Down	26
How We Began	28
Papalote	29
Guardian	30
After Frida Kahlo's "Remembrance of an Open Wound"	31
Bad Blonde, Lucky Blonde	33
The Guidance	35
Acrobat	37
Squeeze	38
"Things Might Be Worse Than They Are"	40
It Is Written	41
Stealing the Dog's Prozac	42
The Men With Tiny Hands	46
Crown Heights Achieved	47
The 13th Fairy	49

They Believed It	52
For Five Years,	53
Sit Down,	54
What Develops	55
The Matter Is	56
Garden of Round Flowers	57
Tortuga Lovesong	58
Photo Album	59
The Magician's Assistant	60
Dental Work	61
Eve's Song	63
Claude's Painting Again	64
I Dream You Died and You Did	66
Widow's Walk, Galveston Island	67
Sorted	68
Reincarnation	69
Urban Lullaby	70
Notes	73

Last Call for Thwarted Love

I've only met one other person
Like me.
This man catches fish
With his hands,
Wishing they were women.
Of course he's a poet
And wants to rub
His blind eye
Against my bum leg
Like blood brothers.
This is the best idea
He's ever had.
The only one
We agree on.
Still I love
This *chingador*
Who takes his dreams straight
Like whiskey,
Who wears stilts,
Who does not love me.
Somewhere in a Montana bar
He starts a fight
I finish in Arizona.
When you drink too much
You understand
Such things, *amiga*.

Nature of the Beast

You unhinge me; bash snouts against my translucent door,
dubious protection. My nearsighted eyes press into yours, equally dim,
I love your charcoal burned-out sockets. I kiss glass.
I yearn/watch: one lolls in the pee of another javelina ready to mate,
others slurp, suckle whorls of her succulent belly, dream
of eating her sweet fecund meat.
A ring rounds the olive tree, they are a children's song.
Oversize loaves of heads bend close to cloven hooves;
woven in a wreath of piney quills, an armload of never.
One comes close, releases a frantic tattoo of musk,
one who might learn to dance, who could be the prince of pigs
in my palace. I could fear him, love him,   fear him.
Later he comes again, alone, ventures from the herd.
Yellow-tusked and grizzled grey he stands in my circle of lamplight.
There's an arrow through his snout. He'll die slowly. Blood poisoning.
I open the door. My hand holds out a carrot to my longing, his hunger.
Listening to the chatter of his castanet teeth, I toss a scepter
to my prince. Our eyes catch.
                                                            We bite.

The Lift

For Ai

Stranger, when we stop
You get into the pickup slow.
Draw your feet in like an afterthought,
Like someone you might want
To leave behind.

The dark is inside now.
You slump, shoulder and thigh fallen
Against me, soft, warm as the deer
I shot and packed out in my arms.
I'm too cold to lean away.

My husband is braced in his corner,
Spare as a rifle. I set myself against the curves
So as not to move away.
When you finally sleep I push my hand
Into your lap, searching for something to hold,
All the long stretch home.

Barmaid Rides Herd—At the Wagon Wheel

So Carl you like me not happy and not sad is that it?

> Yep I like you like you are— not crabby not happy.
> I like you right now until you change.
> Have you changed yet?
> Women always change.

Don't concern yourself with it Carl.

> So yesterday you weren't wearing pink?

No it was more like orange.

> But this is pink isn't it?

Yes this is pink.

> Matching top and bottom huh?

You shut up Carl.
Why are you so concerned with blouses Carl?

> It's not the blouses I get concerned with it's what's in 'em.
> Have you changed yet?

Don't concern yourself Carl.

> How about now?

Someone Different Comes Along

      And by the end of evening you're hot and stringy.
Your Aqua Net hair spray
has melted and frozen again on Ricardo's cheek.
      When you walk outside you
see your breaths make cigarette smoke into each other's faces.
Iced dirt
crunches under his boots.   Headlights pass,   your mouths hold still,
      fall open   collapse against each other.
You exchange gum, taste the soft *carambas* of tamales.

He can touch your slip but not your bra. You'll see him Monday at school
      sure as God made little green apples,
      sure as you saw him every Monday at school all your life.
      Sure as all those boys Mark, Roger,
      Danny, will put their tongues in your mouth and take them out
only for the big game
and to go home and change.

      And when someone different comes along, even someone's cousin here for the Rodeo or Christmas or one night, you love him more than all of them.

                                 You would marry him

                                 But he lives in Kearny
                                 And that's 80 miles away.

¡Baile! ¡Baile!

Bullshit! To start with
Erase everything I've said
Before there's nothing

Prettier than Clint
And Arlene doing
The Jessica Polka.

Forget that he beats
The living hell out of
Her in front of

The kids and even they
Forgive him when he's
Out there brown boots

Shining like her eyes.

There, folks can forgive
Jesse his five wives
Out there with Linda Jo

His sister he always
Comes home to dance with.
The ladies selling

Tamales wipe hard white
Hands on soft aprons

Lean against the counter

To watch his feet fly
Like rumors bad news
Love out the window.

I wonder if the white
Pickups still swirl
Through the gate powdered

With dust, the babies asleep
In back dreaming dust.
And I wonder if there

In Elgin once a month
You can erase those hard lines
From all the faces of your judges

Women and men
Who know
If there was any way to be

Different, better
You would have.

They're All About Love

1.
Leave the armpits of men.
One armpit
    rolls into
    another.
Take off your shirt,
    reveal
the yellow-butter husband.
Take off your pants,
    remember
    other men.
I will not be
the bride
at another Swedish wedding.

2.
Your hands ring
my waist,
    mare lightly
cinched.
My breasts fill
    my throat.
My hips bruise
    on their own.

3.
My Grandfather,
    part Indian,
    all deaf mute,
was sorry
he murdered
my grandmother.
    They had
    their own language.

4.
Used to know a boy who wanted to rodeo
    more than anything.
But I was handy
    and he'd lasso me.
I'd run out of the chute
fast
    as a fat girl could,
my neck
    already bleeding.

5.
A letter that needs to be written,
    syllables of minutes into hours of sentence.
Billy the Kid moves on to Dixon,
giving lasso words
        the slip.

6.
Leave.
I've fed you,
done what I could.
The only man
    I ever liked
        just licked me
            for an hour.

No Silver Buckle

She lost him. It was clear as an empty corral.
Cloudless sky was clean of him. No smell of mesquite smoke.
No taste of metallic blood rising up, gorging her throat,
As he fleshed a deer hide. No singed hair curled close

Against her blonde face. No bed cool as water after roundup.
When they split up they cried together, wondering where did their fast
Greedy hands go, those horny horses that jumped over fences
To reach each other, but then bolted out the chute, crazy wild to leave?

They agreed they got lassoed. Broke. *Chingered.*
In a rodeo it's the marriage of a cowboy's legs around flesh
Rippling, bucking, moving with and against him.
Not like a bullfight where the bull gets led into the ring,

Slaughtered after being tempted, taunted.
Goaded into the final thrust. Only that bull knows,
When the sword enters his soul and his life staggers,
Drains out in the arena, what forever means.

Now she just can't wear the Sweetheart of the Rodeo belt buckle
He forged for her. Hell, they didn't even place.

Oh, Lucky Cows—Grazing Near Big Sur

> After the painting, *Oh Lucky Cows*,
> by Elizabeth Ott, (1951-1992)

We come from such a dry place.
But we honor your tall trees, heavy with swaying branches,
dripping with silver fog.

Our bodies are what we eat: sun-withered *carne seca*, and hard-fried
corn tortillas that snap in our mouths, like bones, twigs, tempers.

Still we honor your green winds, their soft gray whispers
blanketing our sleep.

We come from people that pray for rain,
holding back our tears because they are water.
We honor your vast denim ocean,
its white caps traveling east,
bucking forward; sunlit helmet-headed seal,
then silky selkies, gliding on the sea.

We come from rubbed-down lands
that dream rolling into hills, valleys, and, in the night,
wonder what they must contain in their breasts and bellies. Gold?
Never. Listen, it's never gold, only our fingers tanned brown
and burnished that glitter, taunt us, like pyrite, fool's gold
rushing away with the stream.

We honor your mammoth forests with obscenely fecund branches
that exult, extend their legs up like dancers, then sprawl
open like women receiving their lovers.
Your pines, hands and arms in steeple shape, offer up needless prayers
for lushness, beauty.

We are the children of the creosote
that scents railroad ties and prickly pear fruit Jesus-purple,
juicy from thorns, made ready scorched over a cleansing fire.

Yet, we honor your sweet breezes that taste of honey; the way
your *tierra dulce*
licks us up and down, knocking us over
splaying out our arms open to earth, sky and sea.
Our faces nuzzle your grasses like cattle.

Oh, you lucky cows, who graze near oceans
on blades of emerald, chartreuse, kelly and jade and breathe
in air that rises like Easter morning.

We come from a land of mirage, seeing water
where there is only the driest of heartbreak.

We honor you who own these cows
and the surrounding floating islands of white meringue.

Elizabeth paints you—lucky cows—she is dry as a paintbrush
that needs dipping into the deepest wetness
that is luscious bovine fed on grass. She strokes
your rusty hides as she moves on—she is moving on.

Dying every day from a body that will not feed her.
Not even grass. Water. Nothing remains, but the well-fed beauty
of the lucky cows.
This ocean, that is the color of Elizabeth's eyes, wants her.

But we come from a brutal desert that claims her for its own.

Una Poca De Gracia

On your mantle, a white plastic bride,
loaded cap gun and a covered wagon
without horses.

Cowboy's gone to town.
Your ranch blooms alone, an acre
aching with purple and white iris,
scentless lilac, prickly pear
flushing mauve, half-blown roses
that struggle to be ladies.

Egg-blue speckled Mexican coffee pot,
big empty *ollas* for beans; sharp new knives
demand veins. Waiting in your kitchen.

Waiting for the bride so tiny
she could fit
in your hand,
could live in your ankle,
dance in your chest.

When will you
hang the muslin curtains,
fill the bookcases,
make a mesquite fire

against the Sonoran cold
that clasps you in
its spiny arms?

Sin Zapatos

Look, says my husband, pointing down at my good brown shoes
covered with trail dust, scored with petroglyphs.
Maybe those weren't the best shoes for you to wear.
Look, he says, you've scratched them.

I clean them off with a dishrag but they're still etched
deep from scrambling over white rocks
resembling the vertebra of a prehistoric cow.

This ruination happened on the first stretch of thirsty path,
coyote scat dabbed artfully, arranged in some basic self-portraiture.
My shoes got clawed by cactus rough as the rope-worn hands
I felt on cowboy relatives shaking hands on Sunday.

Later my husband will hold my face in his hands,
clasping the segments together, healing an orange
ready to split, marveling at my oblivion.
You're right, I whisper to everything he says. You're right.

My eyes wander out to lie naked under the moonlight.
These aren't the best shoes to wear in desert with a glittering
mad smile made of glass, bone, fruit split red as blood.
Next time I won't wear them.

Silent Marriage

My grandmother kneels in the flowerbed.
We can only see her head, a black chrysanthemum,
among the purple iris.
We can only see her hand catch a word
cracking it like a nut. She smiles,
her happiness a blurred brightness,
a hundred goldfish, in this still water.

She is wiping a dish. He enters. Ax through wood door.
Her fingers lace together words that run
to my grandfather like bad children. He puts them
under his hat, along with *"No job,"*
"Where's the money?" "House splitting seams."
The silence
has gone wrong for him.
All her signs shatter like dishes
as he slaps them from the air. This is how
the deaf argue.

Dominoes

"*Well*," my grandmother Della says
"*Well.*"
Those are her two words.
One used to answer the door.
One for no judgment.
Only one friend: the Watchtower Lady.
An African missionary in reverse, she
ministers to poor whites,
saving Midwesterners in South Tucson
from a bloody quicksand of Mexican Catholicism.

Alice, my grandmother's strong coffee double
mirrors Della's dense lard silence.

Twins, they wear imitation ruby
and emerald brooches, gold hands and starbursts
to clasp slippery rayon dresses shut
over the deep valleys of their breasts scented
with suffocating cotton candy of Woolworth's perfumes,
"My Sin" and "Emeraud."

Orthopedic tie-ups
brace their ankles
against their great bulk,
heaped up like mashed potatoes.
Language comes out
of their soft gorilla eyes
that lace together like fingers.

Every week Alice knocks.
Della opens the screen door.
She takes the pamphlet
with the cartoon colored pictures of hell
and puts it on the oak-painted-green kitchen table.

"*Well*," my grandmother says,
and gets out the dominoes.
White cakes with black dots.
Ice melts in their RC Cola.
The only sounds: refrigerator hum,
Della's asthmatic breathing, the shifting sighs—
complaints of oak-backed chairs.

Then, some silent call prompting her,
Alice rises
dense, in motion, an iron bell
of reckoning that rings out
our door,
      opens her umbrella
against shimmering sun.

My grandmother smiles at her one friend,
      their waves goodbye,
fade into our swamp-cooled darkness.

Today, two Jehovah Witnesses
make their pale, dark-suited way
to my home in the prickly desert.
"*Too busy*," I say, and shut the door
on their glittery-eyed, sunstruck faces
but before that I take,
for Della's sake, for her Alice,
one Easter egg-colored pamphlet.

Red Letter

Dear Mother,
You are so lovely in your red dress,
red mouth, red claw nails,
playing golf with men's red heads.
You give me a small putter
with a red handle.

    To love you
is to drown in the Red Sea.
Your anger is
illuminated, raging Hell.
    You are the fire
we are always racing to;
fire is called red
after you.

    You teach me all my reds:
Red blood,
red wine,
blue-red is cold
alone at night.

    Does my father
have any redness in him?
Is it hard to be red, red, red
in your family's soft, yielding
margarine paleness
of biscuits and potatoes?

    Our lives are anemic without you.
They dress me mainly
in navy blue.

Mama, did you know that most drivers
who have accidents
have red cars?
They're careful,
but other people hit them.

Grandma Trying to Die

Invisible Grandma lives in my house.
Against doctor's orders, I'm the one
who keeps her alive.
I can't stand the thought of no thump,
thump, of her hand
smoothing my forehead
like ironing. She is
a lumbering slumber
through my life.

I watch her plod after the dust curls, flighty piecrust,
runaway chickens.
She retrieves her crusty bantam hen and cat, Cindy.
Goes back and wipes them off the Kodak gray asphalt.
Siamese screams crack our quiet like wishbones.
My grandma cries.

I lie beneath her corset, housecoat, scorched smooth hands
and bury my face
between her floury breasts and sour lap.
It's almost dark
when I see her turtle crawl
through the door.
In the distance, a blue television fog
rolls out from our house.
There is the heel and toe of bacon frying.
Grandpa jigging alone. We don't say dead.
My Grandma's gone to Booneville
and doesn't write.

Steps

He calls me "Meathead," steers me by the back of my neck
Into a flat sea of plain relatives. They know best
How to make a cake not sweet,
How to make Christmas dull as Sunday.

His family are all yellow dogs, mongrels. In comparison,
He is Popeye-the-Sailor, a dark cherry, dusky in Levis,
Almost handsome with a black crewcut, nose like a sock.

We break each other's hearts so often, so silently,
Only my mother and my little halves of sisters hear.
What we do not say takes years.

Someday Clint and I will bury my mother
Who is hostage to cigarettes.
We'll do it together.
I feel his hand relax, give up my neck.

Family Album
1966

I bought a brand new
old set of family.
Stuck them in a book
and call them mine.
The real ones lacked
class,
looked like they belonged
in a trailer.
I go to school,
write poems,
and want folks that match.

Ghost Pass Through

The day after you died
we all danced,
jiggling our bellies and tits,
wagging our butts,
    even the dog,
to Zydeco,
taking our turns,
    giving you yours.
'Ghost, pass through!' we cried
    and you did,
    air blowing the dog's hair up
from his spine.
    Mother,

last night I saw you,
your white pants,
the cloud of your cigarette,
like blooming datura
on the patio.

Later, night rolled in and out
on a tide of fish-stink,
foamy condoms,
dreams that toss me up
bruising my tongue,
    my eyes.
Your waxy olive skin
leapt hot under my fingers.

Your stone-blue eyes boiled,
rolled like marbles
in an aluminum teakettle.
Live, won't you goddamnit, live

And your next breath doesn't come,
just waits inside.
So you rise like helium
and make us talk funny,

      squeaky,   cry *Mama*,
a deathknoll ringing loud around you,
your round boyfriend,
his sad Chihuahua eyes.

Three daughters watch you die die die
      no last words.
I stroke your electric grey hair
away from your face
hardening into skull.
"*Happy fox, happy fox running through the glen,*"
I sing
to your morphine smile.
A rosary sags
      on the nightstand.
There is no burying you.

No place to put
the cardboard can
full of ashes that is Anne,
      Anne in a can.

Anne to carry with me
across country, Route 66,
      and take pictures
with my arm around your thick can waist.

    You are a fiddle screaming
across the night.
Ghost, when will you leave this life
filled with too little of you
left to love?

    Be a good mother,
take the night,
pull it tight under my chin.
Ghost
pass through.

Ashes, Ashes, We All Fall Down

For Florence, for Anne, for Meg

A cloud of peppery starlings combust
into tabby-gray sky.
This is our season of white moths
trembling in tandem,
over our wasting garden, the last of the tomatoes
huddled, fierce, red cluster, cradled in yellow-ochre
shrouds, yielding to that which draws them
into earth, down.

What shall I do with Mother's ashes?
Orphaned, and without instructions, but with
her impossible deathbed wish:
Place her burnt bones on the icy breast
of her own mother's lost and nameless grave.

I would drive her ashes home, if only I could find the road.
A map that leads me to the rich dirt of Advance, Missouri
has no answers to what mud
covers this deaf, strangled, murdered, pregnant girl?
Stranger to me, my grandmother is buried somewhere,
here. The oldest woman in town says go
to that old graveyard, the one flooded down.

There is a broken down fence herding a small fallen army of
stones, surrounded by woods
sprinkled with tombstones jutting up
like yanked teeth.
I carry the can of ashes of Anne,
a divining rod, a litmus test. A polygraph.

Florence's deaf-mute husband knows. Hell, he murdered her.
Was too cheap to bury her.
Let me not judge. He was poor, two kids left
besides one in her belly.

Did he drive his Model-T into the backwoods?
Dart ferret-like, river-black eyes raking quickly
over that Midwest frosty crinkled earth?
I feel his ropey hands and that frantic
pulse beating in her neck.

I am tattooed with the blue ink of Grandmother's
last words, jabbed in the air.
This story with an early ending. Did he listen? Could
he finally hear?

Grandfather, Grandmother, Mother,
make your grizzled peace.
I lay you all down to sleep, saying your names,
prayers between random yellowed stone,
angry jutting molars from mouths that will not,
cannot speak.

Give me some dream, a ghost sign,
that you rest hand in hand in deadly hand, forgive
and remember love blind of words.
Without your rest I have blood
mixed with ashes on my hands.
All prayers are hopeless;
scraps of words, starlings lost.
They rise like ashes up, mingle,
make of your dust our harvest sky.

How We Began

For Faitha

A wedding ring of relatives circles the white sheet
that flattens us onto a stage
and a knife slits open my belly gutting you
out into the icy surgical air.
Without sound you are held up
where I see you, impersonal, in the mirror overhead.

Still you don't cry don't let me know,
as you still won't,
if you are full with life,
breathing, happy to be alive.

But when they unstrap my arms
that before flapped uncontrollably, shocked
to be unable to prevent this assault, my agreement
to be butchered, you fit there
in what I had never known to be a cradle,
a home that traveled with me.
You fit curled into me, my body's answer to itself.

Dim the lights I asked.
And they did. Make it as if she isn't leaving home.
I made you speechless with comfort, with darkness, urgently
wrapped in warmed blankets. I didn't prepare you
for this world that still startles you.
Forgive me, I said, and you did.
We said this in our first sticky, silent embrace.

Later that day you lie on my belly and I open a book warily.
You smile. I read. We will both always be happy in libraries.
I exhale. I'd feared
you would be a stranger.

Papalote

"*Papalote*" she calls him: A father who floats
away. A man who is a kite. She is his daughter
not by blood, but by battle.

He loves her mother more,
more than sleep. He brings his flight
into their bed and is the sky, a brightness,
behind the building storm of her desert eyes.

He is the kite. Her mother holds the string.

He carries his daughter like fresh cut wood
in his arms to her bed each night. The dog
sighs deeply. Do all men leave? Eventually.
Sometimes? Forever.

It used to be that when the police cars circled
the house, or helicopters hovered overhead,
his wife put a mattress in front of the door
guarding her daughter. These
are his fears now. He phones home,
in deeper now
than he ever imagined.

"Don't let them kill us," says her daughter. "I love you,"
says his wife. They mean the same thing,
don't they?

Guardian

Anna, who else can remember
Our dark and winter rooms,
The bitter men who lived there,
Lips ground shut like rusty zippers,
The women who carried bushels,
Loaves and children tight in their arms?

The hush of them remains
In our bedclothes, in long shadows
That do not dance, embrace, cry-out.
Anna, your voice was a hand that
Crept toward mine when
There was no fire laid, no light.

After Frida Kahlo's "Remembrance of an Open Wound"

For Abelardo Sotelo-Garza, M.D.

Your hand hovers over my mute bones
waiting for the hip's language, words you can crush,
devour in your fist.
But like a hummingbird, your delicate hand is motionless.
The nectar pulses. This current is electric blue with a thick
blond butter of marrow.

You heal, taking a knife, a spear, a jackhammer
into a garden of blossoming, open-mouthed desire.
The pain wants you. You want the feverish, rolling-eyed pain.
The bone rubbed raw wants rest. I look into
Your eyes as if you are brown-eyed Jesus, a fatherly

God. Take your scalpel,
cut into flesh that is inconsolably weeping blood.
You are good at this.
You want to suck out the poison—taste its alum bone—
white as chalk on the board.
So, lift the pocked bone up in the air, it's the heart
carved out of a dragon.
Look, the barest curve of ivory: so slight
it could be the Cheshire Cat's fading smile.

You toss it in a toxic waste container, along with my limp
and the grinding gears of pain a broken car dreams.
Gracias for killing my sprawling fairytale,
my very real monster,
As you peel off your clever, skin-like gloves I want

to see you flex your wrists,
Stretch out your arms, testing how your muscles still spring
alive, surface into rippling brown hillocks.
It's all about strength. To cut, saw and wrestle bone
out of melded flesh is the miracle of mechanics.
Tomorrow there will be other femurs, knees, sockets,
pelvises crushed like shards of ice.

Some legs will have to be chopped, trimmed like trees.
These wounds rise up, under your conjurer's hand.
You know us like family, who are pardoned criminals
blinking in daylight, released from prison.

Bad Blonde, Lucky Blonde

America pushes her camel humps into your face
flings back her fool's gold gilded hair
rubs her natural blonde muff
like Aladdin's lamp until
all her wishes come true for you
and you and you and you.

"*Hey my ratty little country,*" she says,
holding us by each ball
"*Of course I want you. I want to make you
happy.*" The price of love is great
and it's red and black and green all over
like a bad high school joke: blood, rot, money.
Our children will never understand
her attraction; the WALK sign in her throat
before she's about to swallow.

"*Darling,*" she says, "*I've never had to work this hard
for money.*" A blonde, a real blonde, has natural luck
with a brown-eyed bank account and built-in overdraft
And she can kill you with a kiss-off.
She pretends she doesn't see you
when your eyes are closed.

Is this politics or love? In her sleep she mumbles:
"*Vietnam, Iraq, Korea,*" other lovers too numerous to say.
She is tired and forgets your name easily.
Sorry. A kiss
down there will help.
A blowjob, snow job, a messed-up platinum blonde
with smeared hot pink lipstick
can fluff this scene.
Can't it? The world will believe
the televised version. Won't it? Your dirty blonde wife

is perfect when she walks away
and is perfect when she turns around
clear and cold like antiseptic
when she does not know you.

Look at her, watch our alibi
strip and tease: draping the American flag over
Saddam's head (a military funeral).
She can give us a loan
or a vote. She will love us like someone who would eat
somebody else down to the marrow in a snowstorm.
Come, enjoin, entangle with the rifles, sticks and knives,
that are her pale and languid limbs. How sweet is
the meat the Americans beat
as the boys are delivered
like a truckload of wood to war.
She is our mother, our wife, a whore who sings
a song about courage she says that we should know.
She goes to a peaceful sleep.
A lucky blonde goes out at night, fucks,
but sleeps alone.

The Guidance

> Based on interviews with a serial rapist who claims to have been led by the spirit of his murdered brother throughout his crimes.

your brother glides into you
                         like dry ice.
girlfriends won't tell.
                         they swallow seeds
that grow
                         grow into a tangle of weeds
in their mouths.
                         his knife
grows.
                         his knife jitters
in his pocket.
                         your knife
jitters
                         in your pocket.
he fingers
                         your change.
his cock
                         grows into women
speechless as pillows
                         until you stroke them
poor white ducks
                         the ducks are
only mating in the pond
                         not hurting
each other.
                         you are sorry.
your brother
                         is sorry he's dead
inside
                         your life.
her window
                         yawns

as you enter.

on the floor.

is on top

awake

like roses.

inside her. you

your family

he

one hand

a chain shivers

your brother

of your girl.

she grows wild

he is wounded

are bleeding.

jitters like knives.

is your brother.

worships the other.

Acrobat

This is what you get for listening to calliope songs, Aerial
Performer, let's see you squat like a muscle man, grunt
Hard like a wrestler, stink of the elephant's dung left
After the parade.

Here comes the crowd of cold metal fingers, slick
And greedy for your act. You push, inflate up, you're
A balloon. Rise past high wire dangers. Look!
No hands.

You bump against a rough canvas sky, wheezing gas,
Deflate, pitch down to a sawdust ground. Daughter,
I warned you not to leave town with the circus.
Told you the secret

Never revealed. This magic is best left to the Strong Man,
Even to the Illusionist. There is no rabbit popping out
Of your hatbox. Only a woman—who knows the saw is real—
Cut in two.

Squeeze

Oh, Mary Anne, what a way to wake up,
eight months pregnant with a 9-foot Burmese python,
Sabrina, the neighborhood snake allegedly run amok,
Wrapped around your warm thumping belly
and biting your icy morning buttocks.

I read, in the newspaper, of course, that Brad,
your husband, tried to free you with a small dull knife.
Where did he get it? The kitchen?
Did he lunge for the Swiss Army knife
buried in his pants pocket, trousers that hung
empty, senseless, over the chair?

It was reported, Mary Anne, you screamed.
The snake embraced Brad as well.
"It totally locked up the right side of my body,"
Brad said (later).
The snake was gulping flesh
Like she was chugging Jell-O shots.

Then a neighbor—Sam—who called him?
Was ol' Sam just hanging around the kitchen
drinking black coffee with Brad,
while Mary Anne slept in, getting some extra shut eye
in advance of midnight feedings and never
getting to sleep again?
Who knows?

But Sabrina entangled Sam as well.
Hell, it was a good 15-minute struggle.
One pissed-off mother, two grown men.
Well. So much for a helping hand.

Who was left to call the paramedics?
Who knows! Bad reporting! But a crew
brought a crowbar
wrenching Sabrina's slimy sucking mouth
off Mary Anne's jumpy Swiss-cheesed ass.

Sabrina now held three people hostage,
not counting two paramedics working on Mary Anne.
Then one of the captives
—now this is probably the only way taking Humanities
has helped anyone—
recalled how the dragon Python was beheaded
to avenge the persecution of Apollo's mother,
and thought of using a hacksaw.

So the Classics still guided him as they hacked Sabrina's fangs
into reluctant release of Mary Anne, Brad
and would-be helpful Sam.

What had Sabrina been thinking? Why Mary Anne
with her belly full of unborn child?
Was Sabrina somehow, musing on her own
rubbery, tough-shelled eggs
as she kept squeezing, squeezing?

What is a python trying to express
when she coils around your sleep and won't let go?
Did Sabrina want anything from you, exactly?

So many questions, Mary Anne. But then,
you're full of them now, aren't you?

"Things Might Be Worse Than They Are"

A Letter From Queenstown, Ireland, 1939 (a found poem)

Dear Cousin Phillip,
    Your welcome letter received. Me and your Aunt Bridget thank you kindly for the money sent. We have seven Masses said for your grandfather and grandmother,
        God rest their souls.
    You have gone high places in America,
        God bless you.
    I hope you have not forsaken your native land. Your cousin, Hughie Sullivan, was hung in Londonderry last Friday for killing a policeman. May God's curse be on Jimmie Rodgers, the informer. May his soul burn in hell,
        God forgive me.
    The Orangemen are terrible. They go through town in their lorries, shooting the poor people down in the fields where they are working.
        God's curse on them.
    Uncle Danny took a shot at them yesterday, from the hedge. But he had too much to drink and missed them.
        God's curse on the drink.
    The Sullivans are a hundred strong now since the best of them stopped going to America. They soon will cover the whole countryside. Father O'Flaherty, who baptized all you Sullivans, and who is now feeble-minded, sends his blessings. Such as they are.
        May God bless you
and keep you from sickness and sudden death. Remember me in your prayers.

        Your Cousin Honora

    P.S. Things might be worse than they are. Every police barrack and every Protestant church in the country has been burned down,
        Thanks be to God.

It Is Written

For Rashid Kalifa, liberal Muslim mathematician and self-proclaimed prophet, murdered in Tucson, 1990

What was the sandwich you made for me, earlier today, Rashid? Tonight, after you were assassinated, I thought, what kind?

Cheese, with pickle, I remember as I watch your blood map out into some Islamic nation on your kitchen floor.

I watch the stain for resurrection, like the Christian I was raised to be, watch the red lines on the slab tile floor as they lie in wait to be read like the numbers you divided out of the Koran.

You made me lunch and explained about the numbers in your holy book adding up to women being equal to men. This code, so clear you could hear it, told you it was not right to bloody each other with stones of judgement.

Odd to be punished for math, Rashid. Strange to be killed for loving numbers and women as prescribed by your personal, date-scented God.

When you had breath, Imam, woman prayed ,   women prayed ,   oh women
prayed   for your chest to rise and fall.

Now they cry a sea of salted water for you. They huddle on a shabby couch, once your throne, in the mosque built for you. Your hive. Your honey bees.

Today you made me a sandwich filled with numbers I am trying to learn to chew.

I hear us talk of those who have tried to assasinate you. Just as they did your chieftan Sufi father—you shrug away fear, protection. Your life is a story already told, you say. Unlike the Koran it is rigid with calculations that cannot be manipulated.

Kalifa, over and over I watch as you go to your door and open it to a knife and a friend who must kill you.

It is written.

Stealing the Dog's Prozac

Shut up, sit still! I'm drawing a portrait of your apartment in Crown Heights. Your boyfriend's arm snakes out of the sheets, a long cylinder of white toothpaste. Your red hair flows from under the sheepskin in rivulets, blood-sap, girl-venom. The black and tan pug lies on his back tucked under your chin like a violin snoring like a man. The last of the blue stars of sleep
are
falling.

    A *Virgen de Guadalupe* bedspread draped on the wall rises behind your sleeping heads like Day-Glo dawn, her 6-foot-wide crown choking in clouds of imitation gold, her arms outspread, while the skylight fills with snow until there is only blinding whiteness like midday July Arizona dying from so much light you can no longer see.

    House Rules:

    Don't stand over someone's bed and smoke before they wake up.

    Try not to steal the good food and if you do, put it back.

    Don't just put down the toilet seat, put down the lid.

    I am drawing smog-grey rings around your eyes and the blue sound of the shower and your roommate, naked color of a bruised yellow rose, her serrated brown eyes talking to herself, locking the first metal door behind her, shoving it shut with her glorious denim butt.

    Here, you're getting up; can finally stand getting up; drained of dreams; absent of color. You are negative space and your pale skin draws tightly up under your chin. Here's you going out to get more Parliament Light 100s at the corner *bodega* because they're still $3.75—75 cents cheaper—for jesus knows how much longer.

    First, you light your last cigarette and lap, lap it in, letting it out in perfect sable rings, circular sentences, pulling your mink-collared, dog-hair covered black coat over your yellowing white, quilted down bathrobe and pull your dead grandmother's red ski hat down like a beach pail over your shell-shaped ears, and put on your black horn-rimmed glasses because it's way too early to put in contacts, glass in your eyes.

You sit on the arm of the couch and finish a smoke before you give the dog his water and a half-cup of puppy chow. This is him humping the face of his stuffed bunny, Fuckface.

Jesus, you say, jesus, and take Pompey on his Wizard of Oz emerald green leash with you for his morning walk around the corner to the *bodega* and wait for him to make steaming pee and a pig tail curl of poo on his usual corner and this is a brother still drunk from last night holding himself up a bottle ready to crack an earthquake and says: You are looking mighty mighty fine this fine morning, Snowflake, while you light another cigarette off a smoldering crimson butt and grind it into a puddle of dark neo-disappointment, a puddle holding back tears.

When you come home, opening first the metal door outside and the metal door inside there are messages from your boyfriend, four of them, all hoping you're up, up now. This is your plan: to stay home again to wait for a package from home seven days late with your birthday pearls and two months worth of anti-depressants for the dog.

Stripping down to the robe you check the weather on the TV and have a cigarette and it sings softly in the still, windowless apartment air. Pomps is tethered to the couch. He eyes the bunny with bulging brown saucers stuck on his face like shattered Plexi glued-on suction cups.

Pompey is crazy and takes Prozac except he hasn't been lately. You tell him Mommy needs it more, she does, and rinse two pills down with off-brand cola, and think about a job and how people go out the door each day, get up and make it down the street, seven blocks to the subway, sliding on frozen dog shit with the smells of curried goat and nut clusters of chocolate men so ominous you have to cross the street. The men stand on the sidewalk all day. Your name is Bitch, sometimes Lightbright or Whitegirl and you are so cold, wearing no boots, just the fucking clogs and you give up going 33 blocks to the subway full of sleep, red-rimmed eye rage and a ghetto blaster turned up so loud it becomes like silence, you invisible holding on to the ring above like a merry-go-round ride, except everyone is getting older and stinks of hair oil, mildewed clothing and $189.00 rotting athletic shoes and it is no fun going round and round this rosy your pockets full of matches and shaking fingers.

So what if you turn around and go back in the metal doors like visiting prison? I am drawing with charcoal   you sitting down   on the navy blue couch cover   covered with half-inch dog hairs and lighting a cigarette warm like a fireplace.

You make a list saying:
> Buy toilet paper
> Wash the dishes
> Before they come home.

You get back in bed under the sheepskin that is so white, spotless really,
> read the book again,
> the one from high school where you
>> know the ending. You'll call about a job
when all this is
> over.
You'll make some kind of pasta for dinner,
> play with
Pompey, watch your boyfriend fly Fuckface over the hysterical dog's squashed black and tan face,
all pieces of
> a puzzle   that doesn't
make a picture,
but is the design of longing and need for hands to pet so hard they go under the skin.

And you think you'll steal his Prozac
> again in the morning.

    Maybe take two again which can,   sometimes, on the second day,
defy gravity.
    Unless one of those resumes that vanish poof! over the e-mail
    is a prayer that gets answered, a prayer that pries open your mouth
    like screaming.
The *Virgen de Guadalupe* holds her vibrating neon palms
over this room, blessing it with rays of yolk-yellow hope.
    I am drawing amber heat blasting up from the furnace in your heart.
    You light a candle from the grocery store for the *Virgen* and think
about the nature of light and the terrible isolation of
The *Virgen* so far from Mexico.
I am drawing you, drawing you, without ceasing, with crayon, with pencil, with chalk.
You
have a smoke,
    and watch snow
    fill the frame
        of your one window.

The Men With Tiny Hands

My daughter loves, without reason, men with tiny hands. We're sure of it. She is drawn to male hands that swarm over a body like dark ants. They wear wee woven vests and suits. These men have cobalt hearts so small they fit through the eye of a needle and do so in procession, eyes cast down their very short distance.

These men are chosen for their ability to recoil at the first hint of adversity or love. An asthma attack on the way to a seminar and poof! They disappear and our daughter walks, wheezing, crying, and wheezing, to the subway alone. They cha-cha with her in their studio apartments, sweetly using diagrams from the library; invite her to attend the Shakespeare club at NYU, but never give her darting colors behind her closed eyelids, the lusty pinks, golds and passion purples of reply.

Thank God for the homeless man who will say, "May I help you?" when a young girl is holding on to a lamppost and sobbing, sobbing. But his hands will not be tiny enough to hold, now will they?

Daughters, give them up: these mean tiny men who love themselves and their roommates and Dryden more than they love you.

Daughters, grow larger than the tiny men. I dream of you all in tweeds, roaming through a glen or moor, well seated on wide, wild horses. Hair whips in the bright air, sparks fire to speed you on your travels.

Go to the place where tiny hands are made, my loves. And smash them.

Crown Heights Achieved

This is what his heart wants. Oh YES. He, with his smiling cat eyes behind round publishing house glasses, watches his heart's desire—despite all his best intentions not to marry and divorce, marry and divorce. What he plans is to just move in together into his much better place in Park Slope, get married—in say, eight years—not soon and have another pug dog that they can tether-train together so he won't be so freakin' confused like Pompey and then maybe a baby after another five years and staytogether. Staytogether or move on.

Watch fate beating in the pulse on his temple, a thin blue vein clocking each moment.

What, exactly, is their relationship? He is a first new suit from Brooks Brothers (on sale). She is an empty hand-knit sock nailed to the gleaming mantle at Christmas, dangling, openmouthed for a mistletoe kiss.

They are whist and darts, knitting and mandolin, matching in some way, and know this and go toward their future together like Christ. Grim, but being a couple in New York City, in Brooklyn, where they live in separate secure containers, is martyr-hard.

Every morning she gets up and walks the pug around a block any parent would drive fast through and it's hard to get up because everything is uncomfortable except the bed. They both, ah, inhale, deep, smoke because nothing else is possible; neither of them are good drunks like their parents and dope is well, scary, when one gets out of control.

Hard to be HARD-TO-BE , say it twice, neo-neon-intelligensia, *fucking bright really*, in the best way, awfully thin, white, young and whippetesque, with a thousand just-like-you assholes going for jobs, relationships, roommates. It's too much to ask for a car—it would only get ripped off, like the last one did, in a good neighborhood actually.

What is good is getting home about the same time and making some pasta thing or some Indian thing and be glad if the pug hasn't peed all over the floor.

They fit so well, their cheeks downy and they fall like snowflakes onto the big lambskin fluffy rug on top of the bed and dream television, compatible music, really home and not going out until tomorrow.

She is talking to a person held in her hand , she is kissing her hand, blowing smoke rings to her listening cell phone. He is standing beside her, playing angry bluegrass on his air guitar, to make her hang up. He is making fish mouths, opening and closing on empty air, to show her that the pug needs to go for a walk. Or that maybe, he loves her?

What happens? Marriage? Does it mean a leather leash for the dog and walking together, working out the issue of her filmmaker/stalker boyfriend that won't let go and his best friend that is a girl and maybe getting some of the furniture from both families, good stuff.

What do you say? Good deal? Bad deal?

You won't know will you? Is it really good stuff?
What do you think?

A black pug, or a fawn?

The 13th Fairy

> Advice from a much-married *shiksa* to a young Orthodox Jewish bride

1.
Not that it's anyone's fault. I'm Bad Luck, the one who knows
way too much about your past, and future, where
Sweet-Daughter-Not-Mine, all the dirty crotchless panties
your dog waves in his teeth, running through the house with
them like a flag over his head, are buried.
BUTCH IS RUNNING THROUGH THE HOUSE:
HAWHAW HAW.
He wants to bury the underpants! We are wearing the
underpants on our heads!
We know where all the dirty underpants are buried! What a
silly, silly story
& it follows you around the house, nipping at your heels until
you shave your head & wear a wig made of underpants
or panties arranged to look like a beret.
Shutupshutup you say and slap SLAP "ShUTupSHUTuP!

2.
Bones rattle in your hairless head. I'm the almost-loose tooth,
lone jumping bean, a hopped-up worm
raging in a stinky mescal mouth.
I sing loudly, so badly, of a too-young marriage where a boy
throws a knife at his girl. It sails just past her head on
Christmas Eve.
By New Year's a pot of bacon grease hurls across their kitchen
as his former roommate, a latter-day Jesuit priest seduces her
boy in the bathroom, against the curved Quonset hut wall,
ducking and fucking him up the ass while the girl,
his wife, macramé's a bikini. They're poor. This is an opera for
the masses. He will flunk all his finals and never be a doctor.
She will model naked.

3.
But hush. Shuuuush.
A scent of baking bread tucked in my small nugget breasts
yields the next fattened groom, pretty and smelling of olive oil
and women and his waxy fingerprints
left on the women he models into sculptures. The happy
couple finds these women under their pillows, beneath their
bed, like dust bunnies (underpants!) released
from eggs cracked neatly open for breakfast.
Keep your mind on the stories. Notice
how they fall into each other, gasping like lovers.

4.
When I hold your hand it shakes because: Look! Another mad
husband lurks around the corner.
He guts his wife's car senseless, tears telephone wire out by
their roots and the wife is alone, alone except Not So Much.
Their baby is crying and strapped to her back and over the five
miles of spring Sonoran desert, oh they cry, lungs filled with
the scent of creosote, the fecund musk of javelina, all the wild
yellow piss, the sorrow of freedom.

5.
Bless you. This is your first husband.
Your only husband, you say, and whisper his name
into the prayer of your hands. This is the part where, see, your parents give you away. Still not talking, but doing this one last thing for you, together. You scripted this.
 Your friends are weeping with alcoholic joy, angry happiness and—such longing.

6.
I don't show up because I wasn't invited.
But watch it, Chickie, watch it.
Get in the hand basket, duck and save your ass!
No matter what your ticket says, luggage is lost.
Things—most things—go to hell, anyway, on their own.

They Believed It

Gene and Sally meet like rain slapped against sunlight
in a day-dark bar smelling like cheap happiness perfume,
piss and sour bar cloths. Some drunk, a love-sucker, falls
into their beers to chase down his whiskey.

He gives them only advice he knows:
"Your mother is your first wife. Your wife is your mother.
Your mother is your wife." Over and over he lies this crazy lie
until they all believe it. Laugh until they sob with relief.

He holds their hands up like winners, then passes out
into to a lap made of his own arms, like a baby asleep on a table
sticky with spilled promises. Gene and Sally knot hands, listen
tight to him snore, to all their dreams, shot by shot.

They come, regulars now, to the bar, to look him up.
When they get drunk, they tell friends
he's the reason they got married. Before they start fighting
and one of them goes home. First one out gets the car.
The Manhattan Lounge loves them until the day it's torn down.

For Five Years,

our cuckoo, early marriage
    (kisses stopped time, their wet hands went splat on timepieces' faces)
was a pair of gold hearts   welded to a brass watchband.

We took turns.
    You would get on. Then me.
They wanted us to
    finish it up. Make a grandfather clock with kids that chime.

All I heard was them pushing the violins
    down my throat, the beat of a metronome,
instead of the paper lace I wanted
    to wear to school. You got an hourglass full of sand,
each grain you wanted to be a woman .

    Our hearts didn't move,
        just wound down.
We should have been given
        more time
to start with,
    love suspended in distant air.

    There's a place all lost minutes tick.

Sit Down,

your parents are old.
They have no green woods to go to.
The Adirondacks are full up,
what can we do?
They have to live in a Buick,
new, but the seat covers
stick to your father.
He's so tired.
There's no space
to stretch out his legs.
Oh, your mother will make do cooking on the heater.
Oh, no vases, no candles, no rug. No room.
The last of your yearbooks were used for kindling.
Today, oh god, they can't roll down the windows.
I see their lips move,
their fingertips flutter like birds
at us, through the vents.
They sleep a bucket seat apart at night.
At night, if they cry out in a dream, it's useless
to ask for water, the toilet, a pill.
No one can hear.

What Develops

When you move out of the picture,
this is what happens:
my heart spins like a top
in my daughter's room, hums in our bedroom.
As I wrap the arms
of your robe around me.
I listen and hear chill
settle in on its haunches.

We remember you
like a Christmas tree, brightness
and scent of pine
opening in a dark room.
We need pictures
of love: kittens in clothing, us laughing
and the name "Daddy"
shining in our eyes. We aim:
try to capture you
in the walls of our camera.

Tonight I carry her
over the sharp stones and weeds
that lead to our door,
her legs dangle to my knees,
glow white
under the streetlight.
Close-up,
this is our lives.

When your key opens our door
my heart jumps up ready to run into your arms.
I focus: I try
to see our lives in the camera,
developing into a picture
that we will send to our lost parents,
our future friends.

The Matter Is

The matter is, our lives
take us driving too slowly down sun-stunned alleys,
gliding over broken glass in our broke-down Impala,
tracing the southside's old *pachuco* face
crevassed with *arroyos*, cracked asphalt. My hand
touches you, jumps like Spanish, a language I don't
understand.

Why do we stay in the *barrio*?
My thumb hitches into your Russian cheekbone.
You are a defector floating softly away like the moon.
Going home from the grocery store in a gypsy cab, milk spoiling,

meat glowing fluorescent green, I cross myself at the red light.
This is my child, our arms, the speedometer is
high and steady as fever.

You're drunk, give me your hand like money. High, I smooth it out
like dollars. How many clocks,
irons, alarms will we wear out? I roll
out of your arms like groceries.
Why do we live in South Tucson? Didn't you live here once
with your wife
and it didn't work out?

Garden of Round Flowers

Circles of O placed over
Each mouth cup in its saucer

In the throat O contained
And her head aches to fall back

Heavy O so like a sunflower that
Wants to sleep in a night without moon

Yellow petals O pulled loose scattered
By her dream of his pollen-stained hands

His hair soft as midnight clouds O she is
Shy to touch him even as her body arcs and bowers

So hesitant to yield holding on to each leaf
Afraid her shattered green silence O might speak

Tortuga Lovesong

Into warm waters of sleep she swims
with sea turtles, touching their leathery smooth skin.
She wakes on dry,
scorched land to lay her eggs.
Digs a deep hole to fill with fresh chromium creatures,
her children, breaking out of shell into sand,
meeting again in the sea. Hissing. Grunting. Jaws rubbing,
together, in song.

Her nights need these colossal turtles. She clings
to an ochre-amber, marbled carapace of a hawksbill.
Webs grow like viridian lace between her toes. She learns the opaque
ways of deep water: how to fold her neck, her
head into silent shell.

Dreaming she feels the bony plates, thorny scales, of his domed
shell draw into her arms, velvet flesh
deep as bottom-mud
warms them. They join roof to foundation,
hooded eyes widen to sun.

Photo Album

For Arnold and Marilyn Nelson

We are alone.
Only our futures are watching.
Come,
put on your grandfather's Jewish hat.
I will sit like a wife in this picture,
next to you.
There.

At least we got started. Now
your mouth will fill with bubbles
and I'll understand every word.
Your car will race
to our house.
You'll run up
the stairs.
I will be knitting our children,
placing them
in cedar drawers.

I think the grass needs mowing.
Burrs are as tall as flowers.
You sleep,
neglecting to put your feet
neatly together
as you once did.
The cat is old.
She will die shortly.
You will carry her on a shovel.

I will wrap her
in a towel.

Our armchairs
are a foot apart.
We are as close
as ever
we will be.

The Magician's Assistant

People turn their heads like spools to watch him
pound the thick wood thin, his neck stretched up
in a swan's arch, as his fist comes down, down.

Each day more boards are suspended in the air. Only
by the sadness in his eyes, the top hat stuffed
in his back pocket, can you tell he's a magician.

I expect he'll climb the ladder again
and again. Others tell me stories of men who fell
helpless on their backs like turtles,
or of the whirring saw that jumped up and sliced
its master's head
in two halves. I just sing louder.

Tonight I turn your bed down. You've finished
another house of cards. You hold your ruined hands
out to me, too tired to take your own pants down.
I lift your legs,
heavy as fallen trees, up and lay you out
like a dead man.
I get in the box where you slice me in half,
trust is my nightgown.
We dream of applause.

Dental Work

Dream losing a tooth

what does that mean?
My husband is having gum surgery,
which is about
teeth,
about our marriage.
It will hurt
and I will drive him home.
"Bad genes," is what my lover said
about my husband's teeth.
His wife had the same thing,
bad genes,
something you can get your teeth into
before you smile,
and bite someone.

Teeth. I can't help but imagine
other teeth on other husbands.
What if one person
has better teeth than another?
No contest.
Takes a leap of faith
to buy into somebody's dentures, the loss of teeth.

Gums
are what my grandparents shared.
Their teeth slept in twin glasses of water

by the bed. My grandparents' faces, gums, lips
always wet with kisses.
They loved each other.
Not like the way
I drive my husband home,
his mouth leaking premonition
staining his handkerchief with blood,
my eyes on the road.
Later the words. Later the words.
We both know them.

Teeth
are about class wars,
bad water
and trading up.
My mouth clamps, teeth shut,
on words ready to fly.

Eve's Song

> "But of the tree of knowledge of good and evil, thou shalt not eat of it: for in the day thou eatest thereof thou shall surely die."
> —Genesis

You are my wild garden.
I comb sea grass, map caves,
Track the bears of your chest.
My heart is your virgin prairie. You are mine
To roll in like leaves. I am yours
To press like blue flowers.

I will eat this fruit sweet against my teeth,
Ripe for my longing,
Late for my hands.
Noonlight burns and I wait,
To guide you down corridors
Of arms, lips, thighs.

Void behind and before us.
Make love and die
In each other's arms and
Wake to die again.
Open me, pioneer.

No turning back
From our taste of this tree of life.
No denying this honest apple,
Its calyx in our eyes.

Claude's Painting Again

In a parking lot grey leaves of newspaper
blow, bloom up in gritty asphalt.
This catatonic minus-blue sky
would not inspire Turner.

But you paint the aching flowers of your mind,
Add and subtract, figure until limp arms
of a black and red kimono, nestle,
embrace white canvas.

Remember Manet's young fifer
in his floppy red pants,
tight black jacket
buttoned with brass?

Your flowers clothed in thick oils struggle
to attention like that boy doomed
to early death.

You imagine our gunmetal sky
spent with gold, shot with copper,
shivering silver waves below.

In Turner's painting, a slave ship
holds her course.
You grab sun, sky, moon, air,
starved for all elements, wait
for just one stone to sing.

One fisted, your brush
Stirs up lusty winds,
furious weather, those currents
that flow between us.

You stand
full of flowers content to press their mouths
against your salty, sea frothy, white chest.

Your face is round
with spinning,
    you whirl
 burn,
    spin, reel,
blossom,
    blaze.

I Dream You Died and You Did

For Claude

This nightgown binds me into sleep, lashes me to the bed,
eyes closed, into a blindness that leaps
boulder to boulder.

Sleep is a small town full of strangers,
one gas station and bad directions.
Sleep is blankets under our chins,
my pelvis/your butt
welded like spoons. Rest,

you are so tired. No one has slept for so long,
listening for car sounds, home arriving.
Where is your breast, my pillow? I can't go on

dreaming the arrest, my husband pulling the paintings
off the wall, threats to call the police. Sleep is where we go

to be alone together. Sleep is peace in Bosnia, Somalia, Rwanda.
My grandmother had a great big sleepiness to her
my grandfather couldn't get enough of, so he died when she did.

You, love, draw a picture
of our hearts barely breathing. Please, give me your eyes.

I will take them in my arms, kiss them,   kiss
and close them.

Widow's Walk, Galveston Island

Tears stand in the windows of wet streets.
Porch lights flicker: Morse code for surrender.
The cat wears her coat for a 15th winter.
Violets cluster in the throats of sparrows.

She waits for dawn to crack open colors of a fertilized egg,
                     Catbirds to shatter into song.

Sorted

But it's your socks that break my heart
Empty yet en pointe
As if tiptoeing down
To peek too early at Christmas.

Reincarnation

You don't read poems so I am tracing
Words with my tongue under the silky
Parchment of your foreskin.

When your hair falls over my breasts
And you press your face against my belly
I record the eloquence of our silence.

Your eyes pour candlelight into mine,
Try to find my name in a book
You lost centuries ago.

Urban Lullaby

The tree nudges the darkness.
Clouds sleep under black satin sheets.
Cars scream tomorrow.
Flowers switch Off.
One lamp sings of yellow cheese, another dreams
    of daylight.
Your house is growling.
The doorknob kisses the mouth of her hand.
Their house belches.
A window yawns.
One curtain yearns to marry,
    the other burns.
A dog wears the night like a pimp hat
    with a feather.
Wine kneels to be tasted.
His cigarette smiles at your lover
A shoe stumbles
    across the floor.
Nipples sigh against the feather duvet.
Your eyes crust with television.
Your wife's fingers count while sleeping.
Coins shiver in your pocket.
A Doberman nails his bark
    over your footsteps.
China blooms in the cupboard.
Milk spreads in the udder.
Smoke waltzes by lamplight.
The cat tells herself a nightmare,
    her claws sew emptiness into your belly.
A telephone crouches in a woman's breast.
His penis ticks.
The potatoes hold an onion
    in their arms.
A letter destroys its contents.
You sleep. You sleep now.
    Sleep.

Notes

Note on "Nature of the Beast": A javelina is a collared wild peccary found in the southwest United States, Mexico and some places in South America.

Note on "Guardian": Referring to the Catholic Saint, Anne, mother of Mary, who during late-medieval times was represented in images in a maternal version of the Trinity, with Anne seated in the position of God with Mary on her knee holding the infant Jesus. She is also the figure of the powerful grandmother in Christian folklore.

Special Thanks From the Author

Unending rivers of gratitude and love to *Cutthroat: A Journal of the Arts* editors Pamela Uschuk, William Pitt Root for their belief in my work over the years—and for choosing my book as their first in the Silver Concho Poetry Series with Press 53. Thank you, Kevin Watson of Press 53, for taking me on board such a fine vessel. Thanks to readers, fellow writers, artists who inspire, incite, and have encouraged me: Jennifer Lee Carroll, Doug Anderson, Karen Brennen, Jim Harrison, Ann Woodin, Gibb Windahl, Stephen Romaniello, Martin Levowitz, my sister Megon Beeler, Eva Wright and Paula Wittner. Special thanks to poet Jack Collom who mentored me through the process of re-writing and compiling this book—and taught me to revel in the details. Also to Jennifer Heath for her excellent proofreading and encouragement.

Thanks especially for a haven in years gone by provided by the University of Arizona Poetry Center and former director Lois Shelton. Special love to my late husband Claude Bailey III for his interrupted-only-by-death cheering me to the finish line. A big thank-you to my daughter, Faitha Lowe-Bailey, for inspiring many of these poems. Appreciation to those brilliant (in ways I am not) people who helped me get this book written: Liza Porter, Elizabeth Irvin, Jonah Mulski, Martha Chase, Colleen (Thomas) Wallach, Linda Gheen, and to my mother, Anne, who typed and typed without judgment, without fail. Special thanks to Albert Kogel for permission to use his exceptionally wonderful painting for the cover.

Always love and appreciation to Mark Rossi, not only for taking my first author photograph, but also for urging me onward, upward. The next book's for you.

CHARLOTTE LOWE is a poet and critic living near the ranch on which she was raised in Patagonia, Arizona.

As a poet she has traveled throughout the Southwest, teaching and reading her work on the Apache, Pima, Navajo, and Hopi Reservations for Poets-On-The-Road and Poet-In-The-Schools programs for the Arizona Commission on the Arts. She taught for the Texas Commission on the Arts and served as Poet in Residence for Galveston Island.

There she worked with patients at the Shriner's Hospital for Burned Children and developed the program Dial-A-Poem featuring poetry written and read by Galveston writers of all ages. She also taught creative writing for the University of Houston at Clear Lake and seminars in writing for the College of the Mainland and for the Tucson/Pima Arts Council.

Her awards include a First Place from the Academy of American Poets at the University of Arizona, the Writers at Work Award for an MFA student in writing from the University of Arizona, a Fellowship in Creative Writing from the Tucson/Pima Arts Council and a scholarship to study at the Prague Summer Workshop, sponsored by Western Michigan University and Charles University. Lowe has most recently studied at the Jack Kerouac School of Disembodied Poetics Summer Writing Program at Naropa University and privately with the poet, Jack Collom.

Her journalism in the areas of human interest and medical reporting have received awards from Arizona Press Club, Arizona Associated Press, Best of Gannett, The Arizona Newspaper Foundation and other organizations. Her writing as a visual arts critic and food reviewer has appeared in the *Arizona Daily Star, Tucson Citizen, City Magazine, Tucson Monthly, The Tucson Weekly* and, nationally, in *Public Art Forum*.

Her collaborative work "When The Light Hits Your Window," was a featured installation at the Faculty Art Show with artist Alfred J. Quiroz, based on Lowe's non-fiction novel-in-progress *The Apologetic Rapist*.

In Tucson she co-produced, wrote and performed comedic monologues in the literary comedy group Monolog Cabin.

Cover Artist

ALBERT KOGEL is a Tucson-based artist whose current work includes psychologically rich portraits in acrylic on carved wood panels. You will also find surreal environments where wildlife and fauna mingle with domestic animals and the occasional circus actor. He is represented by Davis Dominguez Gallery in Tucson and the Robert Hughes Gallery in San Antonio.

www.ingramcontent.com/pod-product-compliance
Lightning Source LLC
Chambersburg PA
CBHW051709040426
42446CB00008B/790